SELECTED POEMS
HARIHAR VAISHNAV

translated by
Uma Ram & K. S. Ram

ISBN. 979-8-88641-570-4

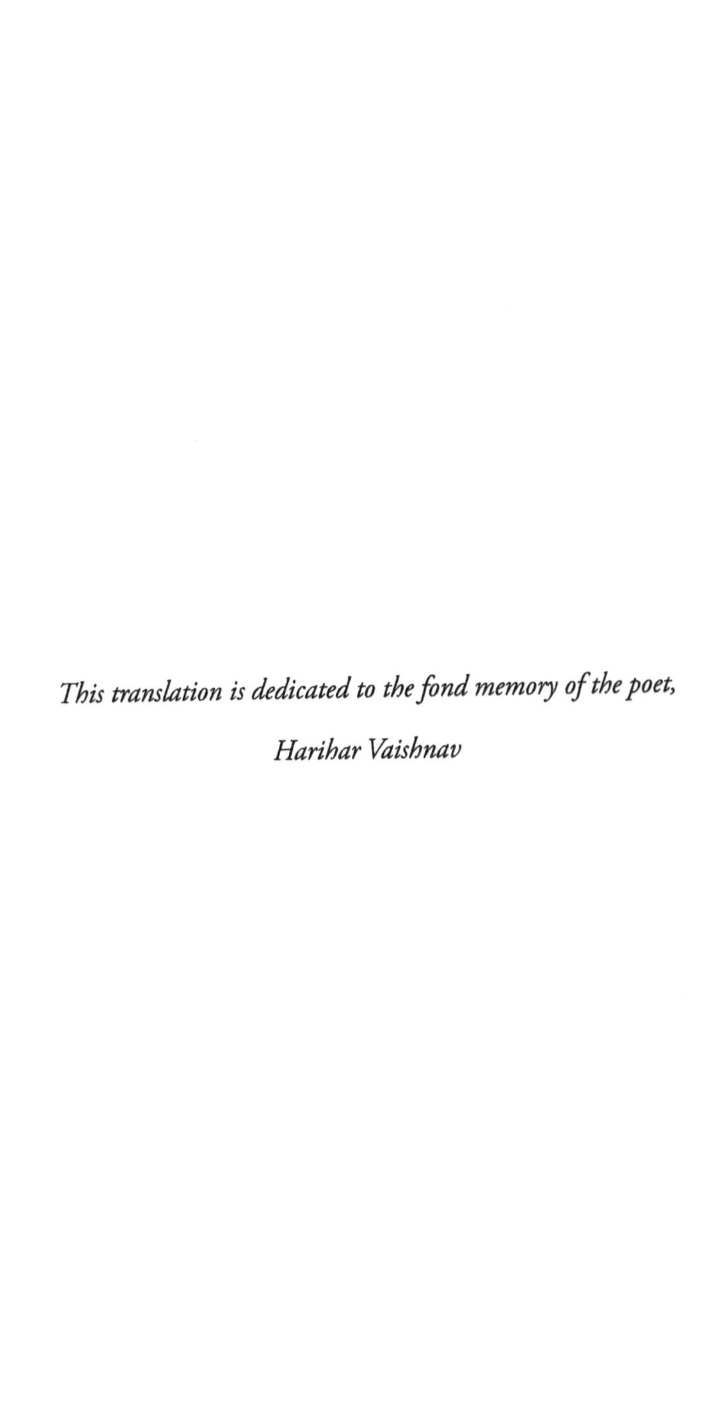

This translation is dedicated to the fond memory of the poet,

Harihar Vaishnav

Contents

6   Contents

Acnowledgements

Acknowledgement is due –

- to Harihar Vaishnav, the poet, who considered us worthy of translating his poems, and requested us in this regard; who had seen the typescript, liked it much, but who passed away before this work appeared in print;

- to Khem Vaishnav, brother of Harihar, and an artist with amazing skill, for doing the art-work for the cover of this book;

- to Rana Singh Thakur for typing out the original text in Hindi, neatly, flawlessly and speedily;

- to Notion Press, as usual, for their excellence in production of books.

– UR & KSR

Introduction

I am delighted to introduce Harihar Vaishnav's poems to readers in English!

Harihar Vaishnav was born in Bastar in 1955. Bastar is in the heart of the ancient Dandakarany. Today, it is in Chhattisgarh in Central India. Harihar grew up in Bastar, and lived there all his life till his death in 2021. Battling health issues in the later years of his life, he worked tirelessly to the end. He is best known for his pioneering work in bringing to light the four oral epics (*jagaar*)of tribal Bastar: *Lachmi Jagaar; Teeja Jagaar; Aathe Jagaar*; and, *Baali Jagaar*. He found worthy publishers for these: Bharatiya Jnanapith, Sahitya Academi, and others. Chris Gregory of National Australian University found a useful partner in Harihar for documentation of the epics in all modes: print, audio, video.

Harihar did receive some measure of recognition, though he deserved much, much more. Prominent awards include the Umesh Sharma Sahitya Samman (2009) given by the Chhattisgarh Hindi Sahitya Parishad; Pandit Sunderlal Sharma Sahitya Samman (2015) given by the Chhattisgarh Government; Verrier Elwin Pratishtha Alankaran (2015), and, Bhasha Samman of the Sahitya Academi (2015).

Harihar was an orthodox brahmin; he was not a member of Gond tribe; but he had immense empathy with the tribes-folk. His poems reflect this. The most important aspect of the tribal sensibility relates to animism: the habit to see everything in creation as imbued with a spirit. Little wonder that many of the poems included here have been personified: the ploughshare, the shoulder-yoke (*kawad*), the sparrow, the river ... all these have a persona. In the poem, *Kawad*, the yoke and the yoke-bearer get equated. Such personification has not been done as a poetic embellishment, but rather as reflecting spontaneous, innate Gond sensibility. This saves these poems from being robust but never banal.

Harihar can be called an outsider-insider to tribal Bastar. He was a free-lance journalist, writing for some regional Hindi newspapers. His poetry is journalistic in character. We can say, the dominant style is that of reportage. He keenly observes something; reports it with photographic clarity; ponders over it with a sensitive mind; and then responds to it in a creative and positive manner.

Harihar's language is simple and honest; and that is his strength. His language is formal Hindi, at times, official Hindi, and, at times, verging on bookish Hindi. He makes free use of Urdu words. It is rather puzzling that except for proper and common nouns, he hardly ever uses words from the tongues of tribal Bastar, although he had good command over both, Halbi and Bhatri. He was not conversant with Gondi, and that was a point that pained him sorely always. He was utterly unfamiliar with Dhurvi or any of the tongues of South Bastar. His world centred around Kondagaon in Central Bastar. The geography of the poems is apparently the geography around Kondagaon. One can guess as to which pond or river or tree or canal the poem is referring to.

The poems included in this book are all picked from Harihar's *Eka-Ek Nahin Hota Kuch Bhi*[1]. There are forty-six poems in that book. The first forty have been translated and included here. Harihar wanted us, me and my husband, to translate these. He liked the translation and sent it to some publishers. But before any meaningful progress was made, his health deteriorated, and he departed on the 23rd day of September, 2021.

We lost a good friend. It was Harihar who had urged us to translate Sanjeev Buxy's little classic, *Bhulan Kaanda*. And it was he who urged us to translate his own book on the Master Craftsman, Jaideo Baghel[2]. When he spoke apologetically that he would not be able to organize any payment for the translation, we told him we expected nothing. Because doing a book on Jaideo Baghel was a dream we had cherished, but before the dream was realized, Jaideo passed away. Translating Harihar's book on Jaideo was our humble tribute to the great artisan, we said. Harihar was overwhelmed. Some months later, he called us up to ask if we would care to translate some of his poems, adding, in his characteristic wit, 'as a tribute to him'. We agreed to do it gladly. Little did we know this book would in fact appear as our tribute to him, after he was gone.

Harihar felt we were esteeming these poems more than what they deserved. It was not his humility in this; he seemed genuinely unconscious of the merit of these poems. We were

---

1   Yash Publishers and Distributors, Delhi (2017). This title poem is included in this collection.
2   *Bronze Sculptor Dr.Jaidev Baghel: An Extraordinary Journey*, By Harihar Vaishnav, Tr. Dr.Uma Ram and K.S.Ram, Published by Paramparik Karigar, Mumbai, 2019.

not surprized. Harihar, we always felt, was a great potential who had lacked a mentor with regard to poetic craft. If ever he compared his poetry to that of writers who had any degree of academic acclaim, it is natural that he felt his writing was subordinate to theirs. But he apparently never let any such influence touch him too far. The result is that when he felt intensely about some inequity in Bastar, his lines flowed freely, unpretentiously, honestly. He is not, to use a jargon, a 'leftist' poet. He has no bias. He is balanced. He does not spare anybody; he does not glorify anybody. He avoids being critical of anybody or any situation, not so as to be diplomatic, but because he has that rare ability (and courage) to see at once, 'both sides of the coin'.

When my husband published his collection of poems in English titled *Bastar and Miscellaneous Poems*, he coined a new term for them: he called them 'documentary poems'. This label had a history. He was closely associated with several projects in Bastar (we spent nearly four decades in Chhattisgarh, mostly in Bastar, 1978-2016) and he had seen things from close quarters. He wanted to document these, for, he felt, they carried important learnings that ought to be shared with the Government and other stakeholders. He first proposed to do case studies on each of these. However, very soon it was clear that neither time nor occasion allowed that. Hence it was proposed to write short, anecdotal notes on them. This, strangely, started taking the shape of free-flowing verse. For each of the *Bastar* poems, he has precise information on when and where something happened that occasioned the poem. Thus, was coined the term, 'documentary poems'. Many of Harihar Vaishnav's poems included in this book fit the genre of 'documentary poems'. Almost every poem here can be read in the backdrop of ground realities in Bastar. To make the poems reader-friendly, prefatory notes have been provided in the index.

I would hasten to state here that 'documentary poem' is not a new genre created by Harihar or Ram. It has been there since time immemorial, and, perhaps, in every language. Chaucer's *The Canterbury Tales*, or Oliver Goldsmith's *The Deserted Village* are classic examples of documentary poetry. It is just that such works (to the best of our knowledge) has not been called by this generic name.

Harihar has generally not used punctuation marks in the poems. Wherever used, they are few and far apart. In translation, the poems looked odd without punctuation marks, and, often blurred the reading. It was therefore decided to introduce these marks in the translation.

As talented as Harihar, is his brother Khem Vaishnav, whose medium is not words but the painting brush and the sketching pen. Most of Harihar's words carry caricatures by Khem. We therefore felt it proper to request him to provide an artwork for the cover. He promptly obliged. We are thankful to him for this.

– Dr. Uma Ram
Former Professor & Head
Department of English
Government Kakatiya Post-Graduate College
Jagdalpur (Bastar) Chhattisgarh

Prefatory Notes to Poems

1. Thank God! [*Shukra Karo*]

    The parallels with the opening verses in Genesis in the Holy Bible are obvious. In the context of Bastar, the patience of God with regard to the inequities being perpetrated on the natives, is more disturbing, than comforting. It is like the calm before the storm. This adds a dark irony to the title.

2. Will you still? [*Kya Tab Bhi?*]

    The voice in the poem is that of Bastar, the place, increasingly being molested by Time and Destiny. Whereas mainstream people choose a place for the physical, natural resources it provides, and the potential of these resources for economic exploitation, the tribesman is bonded to the spirit of the place. The poem is like parents in a once happy-family, now pushed to deprivation, asking their children if they would still love them.

3. One Day [*Ek Din*]

    This poem is about the aggregation of angst, which will result in an explosive idea, whose time is bound to come.

4.   Their Laughter [*Unki Hansi*]

The laughter of the forest tribes-folk is 'a sight to see, not to tell' (Coleridge). The sheer purity of it humbles any sensitive outsider. The force of the poem lies in the concluding question. It can read as part of glib tourists' talk, or it can be read as pointing to another world, another way of living life that the outside world would do good to learn from the tribes-folk. The simile of the river and the cataract has a deeper significance: they evoke the symbiosis of the life of forest tribes-folk, utterly synced to nature and the environment.

5.   Bus Ride [*Bus Mein Safar*]

This poem is our favourite in this collection. Every settler in Bastar would be familiar with the act the poem portrays. It dramatizes the brute dominance of Bastar by the settlers. Brute, and yet subtle. Be it the two children of the settlers who spread themselves on the seats to keep the tribal boy out; or, the new comer, the conductor, all of them presume that they enjoy an entitlement; a seat in the bus is their prerogative; the tribesman must make way for them. And the tribesman does not think it proper to protest. A very commonplace, everyday happening acquires the status of a metaphor for the brazenly unjust interface between the natives and the settlers. The little native boy softly questioning his father is a ray of hope for the future. Or is it a ray of threat? The poem brings to mind the young Gandhi's life-changing experience on the train in South Africa.

6.   Day after Day [*Roz-ba-Roz*]

This is about a little boy in any roadside eatery in Bastar. It was common to employ little boys as waiters and cleaners in such eateries. (The practice is now almost extinct, thanks to laws making child-labour a severe offence.) The boys would serve the customers, steaming tea in winter and cold drinks in summer, without themselves being able to afford relishing these. It presents a poignant case of 'so near and yet so far'. The force of the poem is in the word, *see*, towards the end. Everybody saw, yet nobody saw. As Adi Shankaracharya puts it, 'a fool sees yet fails to see!' (*Bhaja Govindam*)

7.   Year of the Child [*Baal Varsh*]

Thematically, close to the preceding poem.

8.   Little Domestic Help [*Nanhi Kamelin*]

Thematically, close to the preceding two poems. Little girls from nearby villages worked in the homes of the settlers as domestic help. The indifference of the world to her woeful state is excellently and aptly brought out by the girl wondering why the overnight dishes, or the broom or the laundry do not revolt against this blatant abuse of her?

9. Ghotul [*Ghotul*]

Ghotul is a youth activities centre in Bastar, especially central and western Bastar. Such youth dormitories are common in many indigenous societies across the world. *Ghotul* was where the youth gathered in the evening for song, dance and learning. It was the cradle of tribal arts and handicrafts. It is almost dead now because of various reasons: molestation by settlers, and pressure from left-wing extremists. The decadence of *ghotul* symbolizes the murder of native tribal culture, tribal innocence and joy. Ghotul is personified in the poem as an old, senile person. This is apt, because *ghotul* had a personality of its own – youthful, zestful, profound. Defunct, now it is like a senile old man.

10. *Madai* at Narayanpur [*Narayanpur ki Madai*]

Madai is an annual congregation of sibling deities. It has a religio-socio significance. Narayanpur *madai* is the most famous of over a hundred *madais* organized in Bastar. Narayanpur is a district now in Bastar. In common parlance, *madai* is linked to *mela*, fair, where traders and entertainers from the outside world come for quick, sharp business. Tourists also find the *madai* interesting. A number of non-tribal youth from the towns also frequent the *madai* for evil game. Now, therefore, the tribes who are comfortable with wild creatures in the jungle, feel threatened in Narayanpur *madai*! The poem is about desecration by the mainstream folk of a sacred tribal institution.

11. They Know Not [*Weh Nahin Jaanate*]

'They fail to learn' is a common judgement the teachers (mostly settlers) pass on tribal schoolchildren. In the poem, the traditional alphabetical chart seems abstract, because the items the alphabet illustrate, are outside the hope of the tribes. The irony, very real on the field, is that the teacher and the pupil, both fail to understand each other. The title of the poem may well be inverted to read: *We fail to learn*!

12. Barn [*Kothaar*]

Personification of the granary may seem odd. However, this is apt in an animistic context. Paddy plays an important role in the fertility rituals in Bastar. The bridal simile is apt in this regard. The granary filling up for just a short time, is telling.

13. Nothing Happens Abruptly [*Eka-ek Nahin Hota Kuch Bhi*]

This is the title poem in the collection from which the poems presented here have been selected. This is an important poem, generally, as also in the context of Bastar. It is a warning to the settlers and others, who may (and do) take the gentle manner of the tribes for granted and brazenly practice inequity. This was the error in 1911, when the tribes-folk, normal till the previous day, suddenly burst forth in rebellion. A poet who can see a volcanic eruption in the sprouting of a pod, has a true poetic vision.

14. Kamalu [*Kamalu*]

Kamalu is the Everyman in the world of Bastar tribe-men, engaged by the settlers as casual labourers in the business place. Kamalu's death leaves the family shattered. His employer too is equally sad, for an entirely different reason. The contrast between the widow and the employer dramatizes the intensity of rapaciousness of business interests in a place like Bastar. The worst fate is that of Kamalu's minor son. He must now drop out of school and step into Kamalu's shoes to keep the family hearth burning. This is the cycle of loss of opportunities for children of the deprived segments of society.

15. What Can a Sparrow Do? [*Kya Kare Chidiya?*]

It is easy to connect the sparrow to everywoman in Bastar, trustful to the point of flaw, and a singing bird by nature. The sparrow has ceased to trust; it disdains the grains scattered for it. Verrier Elwin, the anthropologist who lived and worked in Bastar, had cautioned against imposing the IPC kind of laws on the tribes in India. Despite being the Prime Minister's advisor on tribal matters in the 1950s, his sage advice fell on deaf ears. Bastar tribes have paid (and continue to pay) the price for this.

16. *Kaawad* [*Kaawad*]

Kawad is a yoke made of slit bamboo. It is used by male labourers to carry shoulder-borne basket-loads of whatever, slung down from the two corners of the yoke. Kawad and the axe are the two principal tools of tribal subsistence economy. In the poem, the *Kawad* acquires a complex persona. It is at once a blessing and a curse.

17. Ploughshare [*Naagar*]

Again, an ordinary implement like ploughshare is imbued with a spirit and a persona. This is not an artistic device; it is a point of fact. The animistic tribes see everything as a 'person' and use lively pronouns for even objects.

18. But, Gowrayya [*Lekin Gowrayya*]

This poem is thematically close to *What Can a Sparrow Do?* Here, as in that poem, Gowrayya, House Sparrow, becomes a metaphor for everywoman in Bastar. Settlers in Bastar (as elsewhere, perhaps) displaced the native tribes and their nests. The bird withdraws to the tree, quite like how the tribes withdrew into the woods when the settlers built habitations along the National Highway connecting Raipur to Bastar. The poet finds that the sparrow values its self-respect, something he never suspected, and he hates the bird for this reason! Settlers always want the natives to be dependent on them!

19. Forest [*Jungle*]

This is another little gem of a poem. It provides a new perspective on forests. The towns built by the settlers are, in fact, 'bits of forest' which, under urbanization, have 'migrated' to towns. Deforestation is not just about loss of trees. It is about loss of society; loss of culture; and loss of a precious way of life lived in sync with nature. The town is a new *avtar* of the forest, commonly termed the concrete jungle. The poem ends with an ambiguity: loss of one form of forest is the rise of another form of forest!

20. Tree [*Paed*]

It is interesting that the poem, *Forest*, must be followed by a poem titled, *Tree*. A forest is not just a large number of trees. Here is a settler, a sensitive poet, who has raised a tree, and so feels a sense of ownership over it. (Mark the emphasis over 'I'.) But the tree is a tree; and (unlike the poet) it quickly gets accepted and appropriated by the birds and the natives. The poem ends with a sense of envy and remorse. The proud 'I' in the earlier lines ends as the 'wretched I'.

21. Expectancy [*Pratikshit*]

This is a general poem, not specifically connected to Bastar. It could be called a pop-poem, presenting a small but common experience. The fact that it is abstract, is both a strong and weak point, perhaps.

22. Flicker of the Lamp [*Deepshikha*]

A common observation almost all settlers share about Bastar, is that they came here grudgingly, disliked the place and the people in the beginning, but gradually fell in love with it. This is what happened to Verrier Elwin, the Christian Missionary who came to Mandla to civilize the tribes-folk, and ended up exiting the Church to live amidst the tribes-folk! Ramachandra Guha very aptly titled his book on Elwin as, *Savaging the Civilized.*

23. Towards XXI Century [*Ikkisvi Sadi ki Oor*]

This is an interestingly structured, and very intense poem. It is episodic. A sister consoling a toddler-brother, both awaiting their labourer parents to return home from work. The history of a cheated people is packed into this commonplace episode. The space of an age is packed into an evening's moment! The idea of 'two Indias' comes through the poem.

24. Crime [*Aparadh*]

Hypocrisy is universal, but it has a special intensity in colonial contexts; or caste-ruled contexts. One can visualize the episode easily. The tribes-women once did not wear clothes at all. Later, they covered the lower parts of their body and left the upper part exposed. Add to this, the factor of poverty. The half-clad woman in the poem would perhaps not draw any attention in her own habitat. However, in the town bazar, she becomes a 'criminal'. The episode contrasts values, hypocrisy through the metaphor of clothes; and raises the moot point: who is unclad; who is criminal?

25. For Survival [*Jeene ke Liye*]......

This poem is in the form of a parable. It relates to a common point of discussion among the settlers in Bastar. Can the tribes be taken for granted? Will there be another tribal uprising? Most often, the discussion dies; the exploiters choose to remain in self-denial. It was so until the very eve of the 1910 uprising, and then suddenly there was bloodshed. In the poem, the title is both, ironic and ambiguous: is it about survival of the person who is alerting others, or is it about the survival of all in general?

26. Monsoon-1 [*Barsaat*-1]

This poem, as also the next, uses the rivers as representing the mood of the tribes: now rising in spate ('the riotous waters' in the forest) and then subsiding. The destructive aspect ('cutting the soil') is 'pretty', but only 'in a way'. Likewise, the gentle flow is 'charming', but at the same time, it is 'sad' to see the momentary spate subside to no purpose, and not inundate, or even sustain. That accounts for the ambivalent attitude many sensitive minds have towards tribes' reaction to inequities.

27. Monsoon-2 [*Barsaat*-2]

Refer note above.

28. Forest in the City [*Jungle Shahar Mein*]

This is a complex poem. The word 'forest' has been used in multiple senses – the literal forest; the habitat of the tribes; the soul of tribal life; and a certain culture, as opposed to 'city' which is the 'mainstream' establishment. Forest fire refers to the growing unrest, including the left-wing extremism. These are the 'caps' toting guns. The nexus of the politician and these extremists is amply suggested. The crucial point is that the 'forest' represented by a tribal leader (MLA/MP), once he goes to the 'city', becomes silent. This silence is not as simple as it may seem. It is very complex.

29. Gurumantra [*Gurumantra*]

This poem revolves around the forest, *per se*. There is a deep-rooted conflict here. The tribes and forests share a symbiotic relationship: the one cannot exist without the other. For the State, forest is a source of revenue. For the tribes, forest is close kin; it is theirs. The *gurumantra* propagated by the State has subtly made a jealously loved local asset into a 'national' asset. The Government is killing the forests that were formerly both, used and conserved by the tribes down the ages. And now the Forest Guard impounds the tribesman's axe! The tribes feel an existential threat when they see forests dwindling; and the politician pontificates to them on how forests are essential for survival! Place yourself in the position of the forest grandmother as you read the poem, and feel the absurdity unfold.

30. Misbelief [*Bhranti*]

This is another gem of a poem! Again, an everyday, commonplace phenomenon (roads under construction churning up dust) is made into a metaphor to convey several complex issues: 'development' which the tribes have come to understand as something the Government does for the mainstream, is, in effect, 'road dust', poison, for the tribes. The road-side trees getting dust-coloured, is the corruption ('de-tribalization' as sociologists term it) that tribes contract when they come in contact with the symbols of civilization; the road dust creates a divide between these de-tribalized tribes-folk and the 'green' tribes living in the interior parts of the forest. These de-tribalized members become school teachers and Government officials and begin to 'reform' their 'green' kin inside the forest. The road-dust thus becomes a loaded metaphor.

31. Wonder How! [*Pataa Nahin Kaise*]

This poem can be read as a sequel to the preceding poem. These 'hands' are the tribes-folk in the process of de-tribalization. They seem to have hardened (or is it innate, sage-like indifference?). The tobacco they grind in the hollow of their sullied palms, tells of the corruption that exposure to the 'mainstream' brings with it.

32. Those Canals [*Wey Naharaein*]

An apt metaphor, for how the wealth (natural resource) of Bastar gets siphoned with impunity! This poem illustrates a common allegation of tribal leaders: that 'development' projects are planned and implemented in the *name* of the tribes, but they ultimately serve the interests of 'somebody'. To add insult to injury, the canal, with impunity, cuts upon the lands of the tribes, without irrigating their lands!

33. About Palaash [*Palaash ke Barey Mein*]

Gulmohur trees in Bastar strike any sensitive eye as odd and out of place amidst the native vegetation: it is an apt metaphor for a settler who occupies 'much space' and is flourishing in others' land. Palaash has too red a hue, and so stirs fear in the minds of settlers. It is indeed amazing how many gulmohar saplings are raised in the forest nurseries in Bastar every year. Harihar, who once worked in the Forest Department, would know this better! The fact that he found poetic significance in this, tells of his merit as a poet.

34. Palaash Tree [*Palaash ka Samucha Paed*]

This poem can be read as a sequel to the preceding poem: it is variation on a theme.

35. Weep Not [*Mut Ro*]

Two kinds of deprivation are contrasted in this poem. It is universal, and not merely Bastar-specific.

36. Magic [*Jaadu*]

This poem darkly contrasts the urgency of *now* with long-term welfare plans of the State. It brings to mind the short poem titled, *His Name is Today*, by Gabriela Mistral, Chilean poet who won the Nobel Prize for literature in 1945. (The poem can be accessed on the net).

37. Flood [*Baadh*]

This poem explores as to why the tribal uprising against inequity and injustice, either does not take place, or, if is seems to do, it fails to sustain to lead matters to the desired end.

38. Answer, please [*Uttar Do*]

This poem dramatizes the frustration of a sensitive mind who sees blatant inequity, who knows that, in any case of crime, all know who the culprit is, and yet, justice is not forthcoming.

39. Millet Gruel [*Mandiya ka Pej*]

This poem is about how the de-tribalized folk opt for the false 'status' symbols (tea) although deep down they know their old and native ways (millet-gruel) were (and are) good and to their natural taste. Worse: the unpalatable tea is hurting fellowship!

40. Man Today [*Insaan Aaj Ka*]......

'What we were, what we've made of ourselves' – that perhaps provides a perfect last word to this collection of poems.

शुक्र करो!

वह कहता है
पानी

और
बरसने लगते हैं बादल
उफनने लगती है
नदी
ठाठें मारने लगता है
सागर

वह कहता है
हवा

और
बहने लगती है
पुरवा
झूमने लगते हैं
जंगल
महक जाती है
फ़िज़ाँ

शुक्र करो कि
कहा नहीं है उसने
गुस्सा!

Thank God!

He says:
Water!
And
the clouds pour down!
The river
Swells in spate
the sea
Begins to roar!

He says:
Blow!
And the breeze
begins to blow,
The forest begins to sway,
The air
turns fragrant!

Thank God
He has not yet said:
Fury!

क्या तब भी?

नहीं,

मैं नहीं ला सकता
तोड़ कर
आसमान के तारे

नहीं बना सकता
कोई नहर
तुम्हारे गाँव तक

नहीं दे सकता
कोई बेशक़ीमती तोहफ़ा
कारूं का खज़ाना

नहीं दे सकता हूँ:
सूखी नदी
वीरान जंगल
नंगे पहाड़

बोलो
क्या तब भी
कर पाओगे मुझसे प्यार?

Will you still?

No

I cannot
Pluck
The stars for you;

Cannot build
a canal
to your village;

Nor grant
Some precious gift,
The treasure of Kharun!

I can but give
A dry river,
Desolate forest,
Nude hills.

Tell me,
Will you still
Love me?

एक दिन

क्या
तुम भी
सोचते हो वही
जो
मैं

और क्या
कुछ और लोग भी

अगर हाँ,

तो
ज़रूर
बदल जाएगा
दुनिया का नक्शा
एक दिन!

One Day

Do you too
think
What I think?

Are there others
That think so too?

If yes,

The state
of the world
for sure
will change
one day!

उनकी हँसी

उनकी   हँसी
मोहताज नहीं
ख़ुशियों की।

ग़म में भी
हँस लेते हैं वे
बड़ी ही आसानी से

खिलखिला कर
हँसती हो
जैसे कोई नदी
गुनगना लेते हैं
गीत
जैसे कोई झरना।

जैसे हँसते हैं बच्चे
बात-बेबात
वक़्त-बेवक़्त।

क्या
उनसे हुई है
तुम्हारी मुलाक़ात?

Their Laughter

Their laughter
is not beholden
to joy.

Even when sad,
They laugh
With ease.

When she laughs
in peals,
She is like a river
Humming,
Or a cataract
singing.

Like children,
Laughing without reason,
Regardless of occasion.

Have you ever
Seen them,
Met them?

बस में सफ़र

बाबा
तुम डरपोक थे
अब भी हो

बात
अभी कल की ही तो है
बस में चढ़े थे
तुम और आया
तुम्हारी उँगली पकड़े
मैं भी
चढ़ा था तुम्हारे साथ

शायद हम
उस रोज़
पहली बार चढ़े थे
किसी बस में
कितना अजीब लगा था
बस में चढ़ते हुए

बस की सारी सीटें भरी थीं
एक को छोड़ कर

उस सीट पर
बैठे थे दो बच्चे
मेरी ही उम्र के

Bus Ride

Father,
You were timid
And still are so.

The other day
We boarded a bus,
You and mother;
And I,
Clutching your finger,
Boarded with you

It was perhaps
The first time
We had boarded a bus.
How strange it felt,
Boarding a bus!

All the seats but one
were full.

Thereon were seated
Two kids
About my age
(Yet, not like me;
Not darkly children
Of a woodman).

(लेकन वे नहीं थे
मुझ जैसे
काले-कलूटे
किसी वनवासी के बच्चे)

उन्होंने घेर रखी थी
सारी सीट

मैंने
तुमसे उस ओर
इशारा कर
बैठने को कहा था
मैं बढ़ा भी था
उस ओर
तभी
रोक लिया था तुमने मुझे
यह कह कर
कि भरी है सीट
और
हम तीनों
खड़े रह गये थे
किसी सहमे पेड़ की तरह

फिर
थोड़ी ही देर बाद
अगले मुक़ाम पर
एक पूरी सीट

हो गयी थी ख़ाली
और
हम तीनों
जा बैठे थे वहाँ

They had
Spread themselves
Over the seat.

I pointed to that
And suggested
you to sit down.
I made a move
that way
But you held me back,
Saying the seat is
Occupied;
and we three
were left standing
like a timid tree.

Shortly,
at the next stop
An entire seat
fell vacant,
And we three
went and sat there.

Just then,
The conductor came
With a passenger.
He pushed
Like an arrogant
Bulldozer

तभी
कण्डक्टर आया
एक यात्री को ले कर
वहाँ लपकता हुआ
किसी बुलडोज़र की तरह
और एक भद्दी गाली के साथ
तुम्हारी पीठ पर
जमाते हुए धौल
कहा था,
आगे खिसक

तब तुम
दुबक गए थे केवल
सहम कर
नहीं कह सके थे:
दो की सीट है
तीन बैठे हैं
चौथे के लिये
नहीं है गुंजाइश

क्यों नहीं कह सके थे तुम?
जबकि
तुमने भी तो
ली थी न टिकट?

And swore at you
Commanding you
to make room.

You merely shrunk.
You did not protest –
We are three
on a seat for two;
where's the scope
for a fourth?

Why did you not protest?
Surely you too
Had a valid
ticket?

रोज़-ब-रोज़

कड़कती ठण्ड में
चाय की गरम प्यालियाँ
उनमें ठिठुरता
उनका बचपन
ख़ाक होतीं
उमंगें
टूटते-बिखरते
सपने

दहकती गरमी में
ठण्डी बोतलें
उनमें चाक होता
उनका कैशोर्य
ठण्डी पड़ती
जवानी
असमय आता
बुढ़ापा
रोज़ होती मौत

क्या
देख पाते हैं आप?

वे तो
रोज ही
महसूसते हैं
सदियों से
यह सब!

Day After Day

Biting winter
And hot cups of tea!
Their childhood
Shivering in that!
Zest turning
into slow ash;
dreams
shattering, scattering.

In blazing summer,
Cold drinks!
Their boyhood
Dissolving in that!
Youth turning cold;
Untimely age
And death every day.

Can you
See these?

They are living,
suffering thus,
For ages!

बाल वर्ष

कड़कती ठण्ड में
चाय की गरम प्यालियाँ
दहकती गरमी में
पेप्सी कोला की ठंडी बोतलें
नहीं बेचता वह बच्चा

बेचता है
उन प्यालियों-बोतलों में
अपना बचपन
अपने अरमान
उमंगें
सपने
कौड़ियों के मोल

देर रात
ले जाता है घर
माँ-बहन,
बाप-भाई के लिये
घड़ी भर सुख

अन्तर्राष्टीय बाल-वर्ष
मनाया जाता है
पुरे वर्ष भर!

Year of the Child

In biting cold
Hot cups of tea;
In singeing summer
Chilled Pepsi and Cola
Is not what this child vends.

He vends away his childhood
In those cups and bottles;
His aspirations,
Hope,
Dreams,
For a penny.

Late into night
He carries home
For his mother, sister,
Brother, father,
A moment of joy.

International Year of the Child
Is a year-long affair.

नन्हीं कमेलिन

अब चाहे
ठिठुरता रहे सूरज
जाड़ा से
चुचुआता रहे पसीना
भीग जाए बारिश से
और छुप जाए
काले बादलों की ओट में

इससे नहीं पड़ता
उसे कोई
फ़र्क

आँखें रमँजते
उठते ही डसना से
बढ़ जाते हैं उसके पाँव
ख़ुद-ब-ख़ुद
सवकारिन के घर की ओर

देख रहे होते हैं
उसकी बाट
ढेरों जूठे बर्तन

घर का फ़र्श
झाड़ू
कपड़े
और
न जाने कौन-कौन
चिढ़ाते हुए उसका मुँह

Little Domestic Help

The sun may shiver
In the winter-cold;
Or sweat
Or be drenched
In the monsoon downpour,
And take cover behind the clouds;

That makes no difference for her.

Rubbing her eyes
Rising from her bed
Her automatic legs
Wend towards the Lady's house

Where an overnight heap
In the kitchen-sink
Anxiously awaits her.

The floor
The broom
Laundry
And others likewise
Mock her on the face.

It is not now that
She has got to know them

उसकी
उन सब से जान-पहचान
नहीं आज-कल की

सदियों पुरानी है
जब से उसने सीखा चलना
तब से
थमे नहीं हैं उसके पाँव

सोचती है नन्हीं कमेलिन
क्यों नहीं करते विद्रोह
ये जूठे बर्तन
कपड़े
फ़र्श
और झाड़ू
या
क्यों नहीं
कट जाते उसके पाँव
जो
जानते हैं बढ़ना
केवल
सवकारिन के घर की ओर?
कर दें विद्रोह
या
कट जाएँ पाँव
तो
वह एक दिन
उड़ जाय
पँडकी
या हड़ेर की तरह
खुले आसमान में!

She knows them
for long
ever since
she learnt to walk
her legs have known no rest.

She wonders
Why do they not revolt –
This heap in the sink
This laundry
Floor
Broom?
Else,
Why do her legs
not sever,
That know no movement
But towards the Lady's door?

Should they revolt,
Or, should her legs get severed
She may then
one day
Take off like a bird
Into the free sky!

घोटूल

गाँव के आख़िर में
खड़ा
घोटूल
रह गया एकाकी

मृतप्राय बूढ़ा
खाँसता-खखारता
खाता-शौच करता
बिस्तर पर
मृत्यु की करता प्रतिक्षा

नहीं आती मौत फिर भी
नहीं देखता कोई उसकी ओर
नहीं लेता खोज-ख़बर
कोई भी

घोटूल
मर-मर कर जीता
जैसे बूढ़ा

ताकता
परिजनों की ओर
पिला दे कोई गंगा-जल

त्याग दे वह
अपनी देह
शांति के साथ

Ghotul[3]

Ghotul
Standing in the village corner
Is deserted.

The aged one, almost dead,
Coughing, whining
Just eating and excreting
Flat on the bed,
Awaiting death.

Death eludes it;
Nobody heeds it;
Nobody bothers
about it.

Ghotul
Lives in death
Like an old man –

Wistfully staring at his folk;
Should someone offer it a sip
of the Ganga
It will fain discard
Its corpus
Peacefully.

---

3   Traditional tribal youth dormitory, now almost defunct.

घूम जाते
आँखों के सामने
पुराने... बरसों पुराने... दृश्य:
चेलिक और मोटियारिनों की
प्यार भरी बातें
चहलें
हुलकी और रिलो के मादक स्वर
माँदर की गमक
चिटकोली की खनक
और डोकरा-डोकरी की कहानियाँ

जाने
कितनी पीढ़ियों को
खिलाया
उसने अपनी गोद में
माँ की तरह
दिया दुलार
आयी-दादी बोड़ू और
बाबा की तरह

भर आतीं आँखे
सोच नहीं सकता
इसके आगे
घोटूल

बस!
देखता रहता
टुकुर-टुकुर
किसी आत्मविस्मृत
इंसान की तरह

It sees before its mind's eye
The glory that is past,
Long, long past:
The love-whispers
of *chelik*[4] and *motiyarin*[5]
The heady rhythm of *hulki*[6] and *relo*
The beat of *mandar*
The ring of *chitkoli*
And tales of the elderly.

It fostered on its lap
Countless generations;
Showered on them
Motherly affection
Like mother-grandma-uncles.

Tears well up in the eyes
It fails to think
Beyond this.

Enough!
It stares blankly,
Like a person
In dementia.

---

4   A male member of *ghotul.*
5   Head girl in the *ghotul.*
6   *Hulki, relo, mandar* and *chitkoli* are terms related to tribal dances
     and instruments.

नारायणपुर की मँडई

डड्डेबुरका-कोवासी
की सन्तानें
आज भी
छुपी बैठी हैं
अबूझमाड़ के भीतर

बाघ-भालू या डुरका
नहीं बिगाड़ सकते
उनका कुछ भी

पल भर में
छीन लेती है
उनका सर्वस्व
महज
नारायणपुर की मँडई।

Madai[7] at Narayanpur[8]

The progeny of
Daddeburka-Kowasi
Still lives secreted
In Abujhmarh.

Tiger, bears and leopards
Do them
no harm.

In a flash
they lose their all
in Narayanpur *madai*.

---

7   *Madai* is the tribal equivalent of a *jaatre*. *Madai* is basically an annual congregation of the 'sibling gods'.

8   Narayan in west Bastar, is a district now. Southern part of the district is Abujhmarh, 'challenging hills'.

वे नहीं जानते

कमलू नहीं जान पाया
'अ' से अक्षर
सुदनी भी
नहीं जानती
'आ' से आराम
या
'स' से सेवइयाँ
वे
अब भी जानते हैं
'अ' से अँधेरा
'प' से प्लेटें
पॉलिश, पोंछा या प्यास
'भ' से भूख और भात
'झ' से झाड़ू, 'ब' से बर्तन
'ज' से जूठन
और 'त' से तपन

उनकी वर्णमाला में भी
अक्षर तो वही हैं
लेकिन
उनसे बनने वाले शब्द
नहीं बन पाते अब भी
'अ' से अक्षर
'आ' से आराम
'प' से पतंग
'भ' से भेलपुरी

They Know Not

Kamalu failed to learn
'A' for *akshar.*
Nor could Sudni learn
'Aa' for *aaraam,*
Or
'S' for *sewain.*
All they know is
'A' for *andhera*
'P' for plates,
Polish or *pyas*
'*Bh*' for *bhookh* and *bhaat*
'*Jh*' for *jhaadu,* 'B' for *bartan*
'J' for *joothan*
And 'T' for *tapan.*

Their alphabet has
The same letters
But
The words however
Do not reform to
'A' for *akshar*
'*Aa*' for *aaraam*
'P' for *patang*
'*Bh*' for *bhelpuri*

'झ' से झकाझक कपड़े
'ब' से बसंत
'ज' से जगमग
और 'ह' से हँसी

तो क्या
शब्द भी
करते रहेंगे
पक्षपात?

'*Jh*' for *jhakhajak* dress
'B' for *basant*
'J' for *jugmug*
And 'H' for *hansi*.

Does it imply
Words
Too
Are partisan?

कोठार

आज
लीपा जा रहा है
कोठार
गोबर और माटी से
उठ रही सोंधी महक
पोर-पोर से
सँवारा जा रहा कोठार
जैसे
नयी-नवेली दुलहिन,
सजायी जा रही
सुहाग की सेज

कोठार
खुश है आज
पूरे साल भर की
प्रतीक्षा के बाद
आया है यह दिन

क्यों नहीं आता यह दिन
बार-बार
सोचता है कोठार ।

Barn

The barn
Is being washed today
With mud and dung
Raising a gentle
earthy fragrance.
Every bit
Is dressing up
Like a new bride;
The bridal couch
Is being readied.

The barn
Is delighted today,
For this day dawns
After a year-long wait.

Why does this day
Not dawn more often,
Muses the barn.

एकाएक नहीं होता कुछ भी

चीजें
दरअसल वही नहीं होतीं
जो देखते हैं हम
अपनी खुली आँखे से

चीजें
कुछ और भी होती हैं
जिन्हें हम
देख नहीं पाते साक्षात्

जैसे,
बीज का अंकुरना
कली का खिलना
पौधे का पल-प्रति-पल बढ़ना
झरने का गाना
नदी का इठलाना
चट्टानों की छाती फाड़ कर
सोते का फूटना
बच्चे का खिलखिलाना
पिता का वात्सल्य
माँ की ममता

और भी बहुत कुछ
जो दिखता है आँखों के सामने
नहीं होता वैसे का वैसा।

Nothing Happens Abruptly

Things
In fact, are not
As we see them
With our open eyes.

Things
Are more than
what they seem,
what we cannot see in deed.

Like,
the sprouting of a seed
the blooming of a bud
the growth of a sapling,
minute by minute,
the song of a cataract
the swagger of a stream
the forcing forth of a stalk
rendering the rocks asunder
the laughter of a child
the springing of fatherly love,
mother's affection,

and much else
that we see before our eyes,
is not as it may seem to be.

होता है केवल अर्द्ध सत्य
जो देखते है हम,
और छुपा होता है सत्य
रहस्य बन कर
कई-कई आवरणों में
जिसे महसूसना पड़ता है
गहराई में उतर कर

दरअसल
एकाएक नहीं होता कुछ भी

बीज एकाएक नहीं होता
अंकुरित
उसका अंकुरण
किसी ज्वालामुखी के
फटने जैसा ही होता है

जिसके भीतर
न जाने कितने समय से
बन रहा होता है लावा

कितने धैर्य से
करता है प्रतीक्षा
फूटने का
कितना परिश्रम करना पड़ता है
उसे
ऐसे ही
बीज भी

What we see
is but half-truth,
the truth remains hidden
in mystery
under various veils
that can only be felt
by delving deep.

In fact,
Nothing happens abruptly
Or simply.

The seed does not sprout
Abruptly.
Its sprouting is like
The eruption of a volcano

Caused by lava
Silently simmering
for how long
Who knows!

How patiently it must
Await its moment
Of eruption,
How much labour
It must suffer!

The seed
Likewise

लड़ता है अस्तित्व की लड़ाई
तब फूट कर होता है
अंकुरित

नहीं होता एकाएक वह
धरती के ऊपर!

Must pass through
An existential struggle
Before it sprouts.

It does not happen on earth
simply.

कमलू

अभी-अभी
मर गया है कमलू

कमलू की मौत
विश्व की कोई बड़ी घटना नहीं
ऐसा तो होता है हर रोज़
रोज़ ही मरते हैं
कई कमलू
दुनिया के किसी न किसी हिस्से में
इससे किसी और को
क्या पड़ता है फ़र्क
नहीं टूटते
आसमान के तारे

लेकिन फिर भी
कहीं न कहीं तो
कुछ न कुछ होता ही है
जैसे
अपने इस कमलू की मौत पर
हो रहा है:

कमलू की मौत से
दुखी है उसका परिवार
कमलू
घर का अकेला
कमाने वाला था

Kamalu

Kamalu
has just passed away.

His death is no
Global breaking news.

It is an everyday event.
Daily several Kamalus die
Somewhere or the other
In some corner of the world;
How does this affect anybody?
Stars do not come crashing down
From the sky.

Yet somewhere
something
surely happens
like it is happening
following our
Kamalu's death:

The family feels
Shattered,
Because Kamalu was
The sole bread-winner.

कमलू की विधवा
सोचती है
कैसे उठा पाएगी वह
इतने बडे परिवार का बोझ
कहाँ से
लाएगी वह पेज[21] - पसिया[22]
अपने बच्चों के लिए
कमलू की तरह खटना
कैसे हो पाएगा उससे
कमलू का बेटा
सोचता है
अब
नहीं जा पाएगा वह
पाठशाला
उसे
फिर से लौटना होगा उसी चक्र में
जाना होगा जंगल
या फिर
ढोना होगा
काँवड का बोझ[23]
अपने नन्हें कंधों पर

काँवड़,
जो अड़ा है
किसी जिम्मेदारी की तरह
ठीक उसके सिर पर
या
करनी होगी चाकरी
मालिक की
बन कर एक कमया
पिसना होगा उसे भी

Kamalu's widow
Worries
How is she to bear
The burden of so large a family?

How can she provide gruel, *pej*,
For her children?
How may she toil
Like Kamalu?
Kamalu's son muses:
Now
He will not be able
to attend school;
He must now
Fall into the old rut
Of going to the forest[9]
Or bear
The heavy *kaawad*[10]
On his tender shoulder.

Kaawad,
that weighs upon his head
like a heavy responsibility.
Or,
He will have to serve
a master
as a slave;

---

9 For lumbering, gathering, hunting.
10 A bamboo yoke, used by men to carry basket-loads, slung at the
two ends.

अपने बाबा की तरह
रात-दिन
और
बदले में मिलेगा
केवल दोना भर पेज
हिकारत की चटनी के साथ

बढ़ी हुई बेटी
सोचती है
कैसे होगा उसका ब्याह
क्या उसे भी
भाग जाना होगा
किसी के साथ
उदलिया

यह ख़बर सुन कर
कमलू का मालिक भी रह गया है
स्तब्ध

कमलू की मौत पर
उसकी प्रतिक्रिया थी:
अब कहाँ मिलेगा
कमलू जैसा

रात-दिन खटने वाला
कमया?
कमलू मेहनत करता था भारी
जुता रहता था काम में
किसी बैल की तरह

he too
must grind himself
day and night
for the reward of
a leaf-cup-full of gruel
with chutney.
The maturing girl
thinks
of the how
of her marriage now;
will she too
have to
elope to wed?

Kamalu's master
Is also stunned
At the news;
His response
To the death was:
Where can I find now
Another like Kamalu,
A tireless toiler?

Kamalu was
a heavy-duty worker
stayed yoked at work
like an ox –
dawn to dusk,
ever ready.

रात-दिन
सुबह-शाम
हर वक़्त

मालिक को
अब आ गयी है याद
अपने उस बैल की
जो अभी
कुछ ही दिन पहले
मर गया था
वह तब भी दुखी हुआ था
और आज तो
दोहरा हो गया है
उसका दुःख

पता नहीं
कमलू
क्या सोचता था
अपने बारे में?

the master now recalls
that ox of his
that died
some days ago.
He felt shattered
that day,
Today
his sorrow is doubled!

Wonder
what Kamalu
thought about
himself!

क्या करे चिड़िया?

काफ़ी दिनों से
आ गया है बदलाव
चिड़िया की दिनचर्या में

चिड़िया
नहीं गाती गाना
नहीं खाती दाना
नहीं फैलाती डैने
नहीं उड़ती आकाश में

पूछने पर कहती है:
प्रतिबन्ध है गाने पर
दाना बन्द है गोदाम के भीतर
और आकाश
जकड़ा गया है किसी की मुट्ठी में

ऐसे में भला क्या करूँ
कैसे गाऊँ गाना
कैसे लाऊँ दाना
और
कैसे उड़ूँ आकाश में
फैला कर अपने डैने...?

तभी बोल पड़ती है
एक नन्हीं चिड़िया:
हो जाओ लामबन्द

What Can a Sparrow Do?

For quite some time now
The sparrow's routine
Has changed

It does not
Sing a song,
Peck at grains
Nor spread its wings
And fly in the free sky.

When queried, it moans:
There is a ban on song;
The grains are locked up in the warehouse
And the sky is under
Somebody's grip.

Under such circumstances
What can I do?
How can I sing
How can I access the grain
And
How can I wing freely
In the sky...?

A baby sparrow
intervenes:
Unite!

तोड़ दो प्रतिबन्ध
गोदामों के ताले तोड़ कर
छीन लो दाना
और तान लो मुट्ठी
फिर देखना,
दाने तुम्हारे होंगे
गाने तुम्हारे होंगे
और
आकाश भी होगा तुम्हारा

लेकिन
क्या चिड़िया
कर पाएगी ऐसा?

बताओ,
क्या करे चिड़िया??

Break the ban!
Break open the warehouse locks
Grab the grain
And clench your fist!
And see then
The grain will be yours
The song will be yours
And
The sky too will be yours!

But
Can a sparrow
Do it?
Think,
What can a sparrow do?

काँवड़

काँवड़
हमेशा मन्त्रमुग्ध-सा
ख़ुद-ब-ख़ुद आ कर बैठ जाता है
हमारे कन्धों पर
और पसार लेता है
अपने दोनों हाथ

ढोता है भार
चाहे जितना हो
बच्चों को भी
बिठा लेता है
कभी-जभी अपनी गोद में
हुमकते हैं बच्चे
पा कर उसका दुलार

काँवड़ नहीं थकता कभी

खेतों में
कटते ही धान
बढ़ जाता है उसका उल्लास
जैसे
इसी दिन की प्रतीक्षा रहती हो उसे
पूरे वर्ष भर
वह
दौड़-दौड़ कर

Kaawad[11]

The *kaawad* of its own accord
Comes spellbound
And alights upon our shoulders,
Eagle-spreading its arms.

It takes on
any load.
Sometimes it takes on
Kids on its lap.
The kids are thrilled
When fondled by it.

The *kaawad* never tires.

When the grain is harvested
In the fields,
It gets excited
As though
For this day
It was waiting through the year.

It doubles up and delivers paddy.
It feels no thirst nor hunger.
It seeks no rest
Till the paddy bundles have been garnered.

---

11 A bamboo yoke, borne by men on shoulder to carry basket-
loads slung down at the ends.

पहुँचाता है धान
मिट जाती है उसकी भूख-प्यास
करता नहीं तनिक भी विश्राम
दम लेता है
कोठार में धान का भारा पहुँचा कर ही

और फिर
पाते ही थोड़ी सी फुसर्त
निकल जाता है
मँडई में घूमने के लिये
सपरिवार

नाचता है
हुलकी, कोकरेंग, ककसाड़
गाता है
रिलो, लेजा, चइतपरब

लेकिन
इन सब बातों के साथ
वह रहता है चौकन्ना
कि यदि कभी
आह्वान होगा भुमकाल का
तब
वह उठा लेगा
अपने हाथों में डारा और मिरी[26]
तीर और कमान

लपलपाएगा फरसा
उसके हाथों में

And then,
Finding a brief respite
It starts for the fun of *madai*
With kith and kin.

It dances
Hulki, kokreng, kaksad[12]
It sings
Relo, leja, chait-parab[13].

But
Amidst all this
It stays alert;
If ever there is the call
Of *Bhumkal*[14]
Then
It shall pick up
the mango branch and chillies,
Bow and arrows
And in its hands
the axe shall wave
Its lips on the bugle, *todi,*
And the sky shall reverberate
With its thunderous call.

---

12   Different types of Gond dances in Bastar.

13   Different types of merry songs.

14   Bhumkal (*lit.* 'earthquake') is the name the tribes use to refer to
their uprising in Bastar in 1911 against the new 'development'
practices.

होंठों से लग जाएगी तोड़ी
और गूँज उठेगा
उसका गगनभेदी स्वर

काँवड़
इसके लिए भी
रहता है तैयार।

The *kaawad*
Is ever-ready
For this as well.

नाँगर

कुकड़ा बासते ही
उठ जाता है
नाँगर
अँगड़ाई लेते हुए
और
जगा देता है हमें
सहला कर अपने फाल से

आँखे मलते
उठते हैं हम डसना से
तब तक नाँगर
जगा देता है
बैलों को
फिर
बैलों के कन्धों पर
बैठने से पहले
उचक कर बैठ जाता है
हमारे कन्धों पर
तौलता है
हमारे और बैलों के कन्धों की ताक़त

लम्बे-लम्बे डग भरता
चल पड़ता है खेतों की ओर
देख रही होती है
उसकी राह
बड़ी ही बेसब्री से
उसकी संगिनी धरती
पलकें बिछाये

Ploughshare

At the cock's crow
The ploughshare
wakes up
stretching its limbs
And gently awakens us.

Rubbing our eyes
We rise from our couch
By then the ploughshare
Has awakened the oxen,
And before he rests
Upon the oxen's shoulders
He leaps and seats himself
Upon our shoulders,
Weighing the strength
Of shoulders –
Ours as also the oxen's.

With long strides
He wends towards the farm
His mate, the earth,
Is eagerly
Waiting for him
Longingly.
A little later
On the horizon
The red ball rises

थोड़ी ही देर बाद
क्षितिज पर
ऊग आता है
लाल-लाल गोला
उड़ने लगते हैं पाखी
इधर-उधर
दाने की खोज में

नाँगर
देखता है सब
तेज हो जाती है
उसकी फाल

हुमक कर गाने लगता है
रेला
सुन कर मस्त हो जाते हैं
बैल
चलने लगती है
जुगलबन्दी

नाँगर
भूलता नहीं
तब भी
अपना और एक दायित्व
अनायास ही
गुनगुना उठते हैं होंठ
भूमकाल-गीत
खड़ा हो जाता है
गुंडाधुर
आँखों के सामने

The birds wing
Hither-tither
Looking for grain.

The ploughshare
Views all
His act gain speed.

It begins to sing
Rela
The oxen are excited
A *jugalbandi*
Begins.

The ploughshare
Does not fail
To remember
His other responsibility.
Instinctively,
Lips begin to hum
The *Bhumkal* song
And Gundadhur[15]
Stands before the eyes.

---

15   Gundadhur is the name of the hero of the 1911 tribal uprising in
     Bastar. It is debated, though, whether he was a real or mythical.

लेकिन गौरय्या

अब
पहले जैसी नहीं
रही
गौरय्या

गौरय्या अब
नहीं रही भली मेरी नज़रों में
वह हो गयी है बुरी अब

नहीं आती
मेरे द्वार पर
नहीं फुदकती मेरे आँगन में
नहीं बनाती घोंसले
मेरे घर की छत पर
क्योंकि मैंने
उजाड़ दिया है उसका घोंसला

गौरय्या
पहले तो बार-बार आती थी
बार-बार बनाती थी
घोंसले
और मैं
उजाड़ दिया करता था उसे
बार-बार, हर बार
लेकिन
फिर भी
आती थी गौरय्या

But, Gowrayya[16]

Gowrayya
Now is not
What she formerly was.

Gowrayya now
Is not fair
In my eyes.
She has turned foul.

She does not frequent
My door.
She no longer
Hops in my yard.
She no longer nests
On the roof of my house.
Because I have
Destroyed its home.

Gowrayya
Formerly came again and again
And made nest
And I uprooted it
Again and again.
Yet
It would come,

---

16 A domestic sparrow, here a metaphor for a tribesman.

लेकिन गौरय्या
नहीं आती अब मेरे द्वार पर
मेरे घर के बगल से ही
उड़ जाती है गौरय्या
फुर्र से
और कुछ ही दूर खड़े पेड़ पर
बैठ जाती है
सुस्ताने के लिये

तभी
उसकी निगाहें
उठ जाती हैं मेरी ओर
तब मैं
देख पाता हूँ
उसकी आँखों में
मेरे लिये घृणा और तिरस्कार

गौरय्या
अब नहीं रही पहले जैसी
भली और भोली

लाख मनाने पर भी
दाने बिखेरने के बावजूद
नहीं आती गौरय्या
मेरे घर के आसपास
गौरय्या अब
पहले की तरह
नहीं कहलाना चाहती

Gowrayya
But she no longer
Calls at my door
She flies past my house
And perches on a tree
A little away.

Her eyes turn to me,
I can see
In her eyes
Hate and detestation for me.

Gowrayya now
Is no longer
Fair and simple.

I try hard to win her over.
I scatter grain for her.
She does not
So much as approach my house.

Gowrayya now
Is no longer keen
In being considered
Good.
She feels that that has cost her
Dearly.

अच्छी
उसे अच्छी कहलाना
पड़ रहा था महँगा

मुझे अब वह
लगने लगी है
बुरी
क्योंकि
अब करने लगी है वह
बातें बहकी-बहकी

उसने छेड़ रखा है
जेहाद
मेरे और मुझ जैसे
कई घोंसले उजाड़ने वालों के
खिलाफ़
और इसीलिये
मुझे वह
लगने लगी है बुरी

अब वह
चीं-चीं कर के
नहीं गाती कोई गाना
उसकी चहचहाहट में
आ गया है अब फ़र्क
मुझे लगता है
वह युद्ध का
कर रही है शंखनाद
गौरय्या नहीं बदलती
अब अपनी भाषा

I have begun to view her
As bad
Because she now has begun to
Talk glibly.

She has waged
A *jihad*
Against me and my ilk
That have uprooted nests
And for this reason
I deem her bad.

Now she no longer
Sings *chi-chi*.
There is a difference now
in her twitter.
It sounds like a battle cry.
She no longer varies her voice.
She does not come close
despite repeated pleas
she does not build her nest.

Now she loves
to stay put in the open
to shiver in the cold
to singe in the heat
to drench in the rain
and
to roost on an empty stomach.

नहीं आती बुलाने पर भी बारम्बार
नहीं बनाती घोंसला

उसे अब
खुले में रहना
शीत में ठिठुरना
गरमी में जलना
बरसात में भीगना
और
भूखे पेट सोना
पसंद है

लेकिन पसंद नहीं है
स्वाभिमान खोना
और
ऐसे जीना

कितनी बुरी है गौरय्या!

What she does not want
is to live with loss of pride
and self-respect.

How bad she is!

जंगल

इधर
जंगल के कई टुकड़े
जंगल में नहीं
बसने लगे हैं शहर में

जंगल बेचारा
फिर रहा है मारा-मारा

उसे नहीं पहचानता
उसका अपना हिस्सा

जंगल
खुशहाल है
जंगल
बदहाल है।

Forest

Here
Several bits of forest
Are not in forest;
They have moved to towns.

Poor forest
Is roaming around helplessly.

Its own bits
Fail to recognize it.

The forest is prosperous;
The forest is pathetic.

पेड़

जब भी
मैं देखता हूँ
मेरे घर के सामने खड़े
अपने ही रोपे हुए पेड़ को
मैं उसके भाग्य पर
करने लगता हूँ ईर्ष्या

जब मैं देखता हूँ
उस पेड़ पर
बैठे हुए पक्षियों को
कलरव करते हुए
घोंसले बनाते हुए

हर सुबह पेड़ पर से उड़ते
दाने की खोज में जाते
पाखी
और अँधेरा होने के साथ ही
पेड़ पर लौटते हुए पाखी
कितने ख़ुश होते हैं

उनकी ख़ुशी में
ख़ुश होता है पेड़
हवा के साथ हिलता है
झूमता है
और नाचता है पेड़

Tree

Whenever I behold
The tree in front of my house,
planted by me,
I envy its
Fortune.

When I behold
Birds perched on it
Twittering,
Nesting,

Taking off every morning
In search of grain
And, at even-fall
Returning to the tree
They seem so happy!

In their happiness
The tree is happy!
It sways and dances
in the breeze.

When passers by
Feel the sun scorching
They find respite
Beneath this tree.

धूप की तपन से
तपते हैं लोग जब
पेड़ की ही छाया में
लेते हैं राहत

और मैं
कितना भाग्यहीन!
दे न सका छाँह
दे न सका दुलार
दे न सका आसरा

कितना भाग्यहीन हूँ मैं!

And I, the wretch,
Afforded shade to none
Love to none
Shelter to none!

Oh! the wretch, I!

प्रतीक्षित

प्रतीक्षारत दृष्टि
दूर देहरी
देहरी के उस पार
न जाने कहाँ तक
जा कर

हर बार
लौट आती निराश
आहट पा थोड़ी-सी भी
धड़क उठता हृदय
बढ़ जाती धड़कन
दिल की हर बार

क्योंकि शायद
अप्रत्याशित
कल्पनातीत
को आज होना था
प्रत्याशित
बनना था साकार

लेकिन
अन्ततः वही हुआ
कल्पनातीत
साकार न हुआ
अप्रत्याशित

Expectancy

Expectant eye
Looking far away
Across the portal
Far, far away
Sees

And returns disappointed
Every time
A slight sound
And the heart leaps up
The heartbeat rises
Every time

Because perhaps
The unexpected
Beyond imagination
Was to become
Real today

But
At last, what happened was
That the beyond-imagination
Did not turn real;
The unexpected

प्रत्याशित न बना
और
पथरा गयीं आँखें
जो थीं प्रतीक्षारत

Did not become the expected
And
The expectant eyes
Turned tired.

दीपशिखा

दीये की टिमटिमाती लौ
को देख कर
तुमने यही तो कहा न उस दिन
कि
यह दीया
न रह पायेगा
आलोकित अधिक देर तक
न कर पायेगा दूर
निविड़ तम को पर्याप्त सक्षमता से

तुमने ही तो कहा था न
कि इस दीये की लौ में
नहीं वह ताब कि
वह प्रकाशित हो
तुम्हारे पथ में
पहुँचा सके
तुम्हें, तुम्हारे गंतव्य तक

और

तुम्हें हो सकेगी प्राप्ति
उस चरम सुख की
तुम जिये जा रहे हो

जिसकी अपेक्षा में

Flicker of the Lamp

Seeing
The flickering flame of a lamp
Is this not what you said that day
That
This lamp
Cannot last
For long,
It lacks the ability
To dispel distant darkness.

You it was had averred
That this lamp
Does not have the brightness
Enough to light the path
To reach you
To your destination.

For you

To attain
To that supreme bliss
For which you are
Hoping, striving.

But
Are you yet not convinced
That the lamp you had dubbed

लेकिन
क्या तुम्हें अब भी
नहीं है अहसास
इस तथ्य का
कि जिस दीये को तुमने
अयोग्य, आलोकहीन
और न जाने
कितनी अर्थ-हीन, बेतुकी
संज्ञाएँ दी थीं
वही दीप
कर रहा है आलोकित
आज भी तुम्हारे पथ को

उसी दीये ने आज
कर रखा है उन्नत
तुम्हारे शीश को
जिसके बल पर तुम
हो गये हो सफल
पाने की अपना लक्ष्य

फिर भी
कोस रहे हो
उसी दीप को

अन्ततः
तुम क्या सोच रहे हो?

As useless, dull
And what not
Irrelevant, nonsense names
Is still lighting up your path?

That same lamp today
Is cheering up your face
On whose strength
You have succeeded
In reaching your goal!

And yet
You curse
That lamp!

After all
What are you thinking?

इक्कीसवीं सदी की ओर

उघड़े बदन बच्चों की निगाहें
लगी हैं
इक्कीसवीं सदी की ओर
भूखा पेट वर्तमान
ताक रहा है भविष्य की ओर
कि भर जाएगा पेट
नहीं रहेंगे बदन उघड़े
कमाने गए हैं आया-बुबा
लौटेंगे इक्कीसवीं सदी में
हँसी-खुशी का ले कर झुनझुना

आयती अपने नानी भाई
चमरू को
दे रही है सान्त्वना
मत रो बाबू
चुप रह, बहुत हो गया रोना

चमरू नन्हा-सा है तो क्या
समझता है भुलावे की भाषा
जानता है अतीत को
भोग रहा है वर्तमान

और
नहीं है उसे भविष्य की आशा
आयती भी समझती है
सब-कुछ

Towards XXI Century

Famished children
Have their eyes
On the twenty-first century.
Hungry present
Is staring at the future
Hoping for a full stomach;
Freedom from famished bodies.
Mother and father
Have gone to work
They will return in the twenty-first century
With a bauble of joy and laughter.

Aayati is consoling
Her little sibling Chamaru:
Don't cry
Now quiet, enough of crying.

Chamaru is a toddler
But can tell
False consolation.
He knows the past
He is suffering the present
And
He expects nothing from future.

पर क्या करे, बड़ी है
कैसे कह दे सच,
कि सच है बड़ा कड़वा
उसका दायित्व है
नानी को भुलकाना

दे रही है कब से
वह उसे सान्त्वना।

Aayati also knows it well
But she is senior;
How can she utter the truth
That truth that is bitter?
She is responsible;
She must befool her sibling.

She continues
to console him.

अपराध

जब कभी
कोई औरत
बाज़ार से
उघड़े बदन
गुज़र रही होती है
और लागों की
नज़र पड़ती है उस पर

तब
कई लोग छोड़ कर खरीददारी
लपकते हैं उस ओर
वह औरत
सहम कर
दूर जाने की करती है उपक्रम
लोग पकड़ लेते हैं
उसे, आरोप लगा कर अश्लीलता का
देते हैं धमकी
पुलिस-थाने ले जाने की

वह डर जाती है
तब लोग उसे
बहला कर सबके देखते
ले जाते हैं अपने साथ
यह कह कर कि चलो,
हम कर देंगे कपड़ों का बन्दोबस्त
तुम्हारे लिये

Crime

Whenever
A woman
Is seen passing through the bazar
Half-clad
She grabs people's attention,

Many there are that drop their shopping
And hurry towards her.

Shocked, that woman
Tries to distance away.
People grab her,
Charge her with indecency,
And throw threats
They will drag her to the police.

She is terrified.
People then soothe her
And even as all watch,
They talk her away
To organize clothes for her.

चली जाती है
वह औरत उनके साथ
दूर जाते ही बाजार से
टूट पड़ते हैं लोग उस पर
पहले उघड़े बदन थी वह अकेली
अब
सब लोग नंगे हो जाते हैं।

She accompanies them.
Once away from the bazar
People pounce upon her.

Earlier, she was half-clad,
Now, all are naked.

जीने के लिए

सूरज निकल आया था
मैंने जा कर उन्हें बताया
भाई! उठो
निकल चुका है सूरज
यानी जा चुकी है रात
आ गया है दिन

लोगों ने डाँटा मुझे
पागल हो गये हो तुम!
तुम्हारे कहने से
कैसे निकल सकता है दिन
अभी सुबह होने का
बजा कहाँ है भोंपू

मैंने कहा
भोंपू बजाने वाले तो
सोये पड़े है खुद

लोगों ने मेरे गाल पर
मारी चपत
यह कह कर भगा दिया
कि उनके विरुद्ध
बोलने का साहस

For Survival

The sun had risen.
I went and admonished them
Brothers! Arise
The sun has risen
The night is past
The day is on!

People reproached me –
Are you mad?
The day cannot break
Just because you say so;
Has the hooter sounded
To announce day-break?

I said
The hooter-men
Are asleep.

People slapped me
On my cheek.
They chased me away –
How dare you counter us,
They queried.
Their words
Are dissolved in our blood.

कैसे कर सके हो तुम?
उनकी बातें
रच-बस गयी हैं
हमारे खून में

हमने माना है आज तक
उनका कहा
आज कैसे मान लें
तुम्हारी बात?

जीना है
और दुनिया में रहना है तो
जाओं अभी
घुस जाओ बिस्तर में
और प्रतीक्षा करो
भोंपू के बजने की।

We have conformed
To whatever they have said
Now how can we accept
Your words?

If you have to survive
In the world
Then better go
And slip into your couch
And wait
For the hooter's call.

बरसातः एक

बरसात में
उफनती नदियों का बहना
वैसे तो बड़ा अच्छा लगता है
लेकिन तब बड़ा बुरा भी लगता है
जब उसका उफान
पड़ जाता है ठण्डा
कुछ ही देर में

तब बड़ा भला लगता है
जंगल के बीच से गुजरती
पानी से लबालब भरी नदी को देखना
जो बह रही होती है
बडी ही मन्थर गति से
तब लगता है
क्यों न हम उसके सुरम्य तट पर
बैठ कर आल्हादित हो लें
और गाएँ कोई
प्यार भरा आत्मीय गीत

दरअसल
हर नदी
हर उफनती नदी की
अंततः यही नियति होती है।
और वस्तुतः
वह इसी स्थिति में
बड़ी भली लगती है।

Monsoon-1

The sight of rivers
In spate during rains
Is pretty in a way,
But it is sad when
The spate recedes
Shortly.

Then it is a pretty sight
To see the full river
Wading through the forest;
Now flowing gently;
Then you feel
Like sitting on its bank
In ecstasy
To sing a song of love!

In fact,
Every river
Every river in spate
Must eventually end thus,
And truly
It is thus that it looks
Charming.

बरसातः दो

जंगल के बीच से
गुजरते हुए
दिख जाते हैं
कई बरसाती नाले
और पानी की बेतरतीब
बहती धारा
कटाव करती हुई
आसपास की ज़मीन का
मुझे अच्छा लगता है
उन्हें देखना

कई जगह
वे धाराएँ जब
दिख जाती हैं
बनाती हुई छोटे - छोटे प्रपात
शिला - खण्ड पर बराबर
गिरती हुई
और उन्हें बदलती हुई
रेत के कणों में
तब मैं सोचता हूँ
इन्हें ऐसे ही बहते रहना चाहिए

यही धाराएँ
आगे चलकर बनाएँगी
बड़ी-बड़ी नदियाँ
और प्रपात

Monsoon-2

Several seasonal rapids
Are seen wading through
The forest,
The riotous waters
Cutting the soil
at the edges.
I like to watch
That.

At places where
The rapids
Fall as cataracts
Upon hard rock,
Eroding it
Into sand grains,
I get a thought:
May such flow endure!

The streams shall
In due course
Form large rivers
And water falls.

I do not know why
But I feel an urge
To reach out to them

मुझे पता नहीं क्यों
तब लगने लगता है
कि उन्हें, उनके पास जा कर
अपने गले से लगा लूँ
और प्यार करूँ
अपनी लाड़ली बेटी की तरह
उस वक़्त
मेरे भीतर भी कहीं
फूट रहे होते हैं
सोते
बह रही होती है
कोई नदी
और बन रहे होते हैं
प्रपात।

And gather them in a hug
And shower my love on them
As on a darling daughter
At such moments.
Somewhere within me
Some dormant streams
Spring up,
And some river gushes forth
To form water-falls.

जंगल शहर में

जंगल में आग
फैल रही है
फैलती ही जा रही है
तेजी से

ज़मीन नापते ज़रीब
गुम हो जाते हैं
जंगल में
पेड़ काटते धारदार आरे
हो जाते हैं भोथरे
लट्ठों से भरी ट्रकें
ख़ाली करवा ली जाती है।
कूपों के आसपास
निगरानी करते हैं
ज़िन्दा पेड़

होती है घोषणा
नहीं कटेंगे पेड़
आज के बाद
नहीं
नहीं काटने देंगे
अब और ज़्यादा
तब
इन घोषणाओं से डर कर
एक दिन
कई टोपियाँ

Forest in the City

There is a fire
Spreading in the forest,
Spreading fast!

They that measure land
Get lost in the forest;
The saws that hew the trees
Go blunt;
Bales in the trucks
Are offloaded
Around the forest coupes.
Live trees stand guard.

It is declared:
No more felling of trees,
Now on we shall not suffer
Felling of trees!
Then
Awed by such declaration
One day
In the inky night hour
Toting guns
Several caps descend
Upon the *ghotul,*
Led by a big cap,

रात के स्याह अँधेरे में
बन्दूकें ताने
पहुँच जाती हैं
घोटूल के पास
एक बड़ी टोपी के नेतृत्व में
और एक तेज रोशनी
पड़ती है
ठीक घोटुल के ऊपर
और
अनायास ही बज उठती हैं तोड़ियाँ
जिनकी आवाज़
गूँज जाती है
जंगली हवाओं में मिल कर
कोसों दूर तक

बात ही बात में
जुट जाता है जंगल
पूरा का पूरा जंगल

इधर
तोड़ियों की आवाज से
हो जाता है चौकन्ना
दूसरा एक घोटुल

इन सारी बातों से बेख़बर टोपियाँ
बढ़ती हैं घोटुल की ओर
रास्ते में
मिल जाता है समूचा जंगल
तब बदहवासी में
लौटती हैं टोपियाँ

And a strong beam
Of light strikes upon the *ghotul,*
And all at once the drums begin to beat
And their sound echoes
With the forest wind
Far, far away.

Anon, the forest unites,
The entire forest unites.

Here
Drumbeats
Alert another *ghotul.*

Unconcerned with all of this,
The caps march upon the *ghotul*
And they come upon the full forest
On their way.

Then, confused,
The caps return to their heads.
On the way they confront
Another forest
And the guns roar
And the forest scatters
Amidst the gunfire sound.

The caps flee
And hide within their boxes
And lock themselves

अपने सिरों की ओर
कि रासते में
फिर मिल जाता है
एक जंगल
और बज उठती हैं बन्दूकें
बिखर जाता है जंगल
बन्दूकों की आवाज़ से

टोपियाँ भाग आती हैं वापस
घुस जाती हैं सन्दूकों में
बन्द कर लेती हैं ताले
किसी से कुछ भी
नहीं कहतीं
चाबियों के कानों तक भी
पहुँच नहीं पाती वारदात की तफ़सील

फिर आता है
देश का बत्तीसवाँ गणतन्त्र-दिवस

जंगल का ही एक टुकड़ा
सफ़ेद खादी की थान में लिपटा
आता है उस रोज़
लेकिन बात नहीं करता वह
उस समूचे जंगल से

दो-तीन मील दूर
एक ख़वाबगाह में
बड़ी-बड़ी कुर्सियों
और मसनदों के बीच घिरा
ले रहा होता है जायज़ा

Mentioning nothing to anybody;
Even the ears of the keys
Receive no report.

And then comes
The thirty-second Republic Day!

A part of the forest
Adorned in white khadi
Comes that day
But with the entire forest
He speaks nothing.

A couple of miles away
In a dream-house
Amidst large chairs
And bolsters
He is reviewing,
Sharing of the loot.

Just then,
Trucks laden with sacks
Of tamarind and *sal*-seeds
And *kullu* or *sal*-incense.

Just then
A mid-rung cap
With two flowers
Arrives in disarray
Towards a large chair:

भाटों की तुकबन्दियों का
देखते हुए
लद्दों से भरी ट्रकें
इमली, सालबीज
और कुल्लू या साल-धूप के बोरे

तभी एक मँझली टोपी
दो फूल खोंसे
बदहवास-सी पहुँचती है
एक बड़ी कुर्सी के पास:
कुर्सी-कुर्सी
जंगल घुस आया है शहर में
टोपियाँ घेर ली गयी हैं

बेचारी टोपी काँप रही होती है।
थर-थर
बाक़ी सभी कुर्सियाँ,
मसनदें हँस पड़ती हैं

जंगल का वह एक अदद टुकड़ा भी
महुआ की जगह खाता हुआ अंगूर
कर उठता है अट्टहास:
पागल हो गयी है टोपी
जंगल कभी घुस सकता है
शहर में भला?

पर गिड़गिड़ाती है
दो फूल खोंसी हुई वह मँझली टोपी
सभी चल पड़ते हैं
शहर की ओर
वहाँ, उस जंगल की

Chair, chair,
The forest has invaded the city;
The caps are under seize!

The hapless cap is trembling
The other chairs and bolsters
Burst out laughing!

The important part of the forest,
Munching on grapes instead of mahua,
Also bursts out laughing:
The cap is mad,
Can forest ever invade a city?

That mid-rung cap with two flowers
Grumbles.
All set forth towards the city
There, one hears a single voice of the forest:
What shall we gain
Mingling with chairs and bolsters?
We want that part of ours
We want that tree
We would like to talk today with that,
Only with that
Felling which
It is put to use in some building.

Then, do not know why
But that part of the forest
Does not sing a *rela*
Nor a *hulki*

केवल एक ही आवाज़ सुनायी पड़ती है:
क्या करेंगे हम
कुर्सियों या मसनदों से मिल कर
हमें हमारा वह टुकड़ा
वह पेड़ चाहिये
हम आज बात करना चाहते हैं
उसी से, केवल उसी से
जिसे काट कर
किसी इमारत में
लगाने का काम
कर दिया गया है शुरू

तब पता नहीं क्यों
जंगल का वह टुकड़ा
रेला नहीं गाता
या हुलकी भी
केवल बचाते हुए
अपना सफ़ेद खादी का थान
भाग खड़ा होता है
शहर के आख़िर में बने
कबूतरख़ाने की ओर

और एक काला कोट
जंगल को देता है आदेश
लौट जाने की वापस
अपनी जगह।

It just slips away
Guarding its white khadi
Towards the pigeon-hole
At the city's end.

And a dark coat
Orders the forest
To return to its place.

गुरुमंत्र

हर साल
काट लिए जाते हैं
भीमकाय पेड़
बेरहमी से
साल और सागौन के
और
व्यापारिक डिपों से
नीलामी कर दिये जाते हैं रोज़

ट्रकें ले जाती हैं
लाद कर
आरा मशीनें
चीरती है बड़े-बड़े शरीर
फिर
बन जाते हैं ये
बड़ी-बड़ी इमारतें

तब हिड़मा या मँगलू
चीखता है:
जंगल नहीं तुम्हारे बाप का
नहीं लगाए थे
ये पेड़ तुमने
दब जाती है
उसकी आवाज़
नीलाम की बोलियों में

Gurumantra

Every year
Huge trees
Of *sal*[17] and teak
Are hewn down
And
Auctioned everyday
from the commercial depot.

The trucks
Bear them away.
Saw mills
Split the torso
That later
Become parts
Of large buildings.

Hidma and Manglu
Yell:
The forest does not belong
to your father
Nor had you planted these trees.

---

17 *Shorea Robusta. Sal* is a tree celebrated in the Ramayana, when Rama was in exile in the Dandakaranya, and pierced seven *sal* trees with a single shaft, just to convince Sugriva of his (Rama's) prowess.

या कि मशीनों की घरघराहट में
और चीख़ती है।
सोनाय, सुदनी या कि मनची
अपने नातियों के साथ
महुआ या टोरा
सालबीज या चार बीनती
क्या होगा हमारे पेट का
हमारी छत का
क्यों कर रहे हो तुम हमें नंगे

उसकी चीख़
डूब जाती है
खुरसेल[34] की घाटियों से
गुज़रती ट्रकों की कर्कश आवाज़ में
ट्रकें, जो जाती हैं
धमतरी, रायपुर, विशापापटनम्

तब आती है उनके गाँव में
एक बड़ी कुर्सी
अपने तमाम तामझाम के साथ
सब जुड़ जाते हैं
घोटूल में
बड़े-बूढ़े सभी
उस बड़ी कुर्सी को रिझाने के लिये

'माँदरी - नृत्य' का होता है आयोजन
फिर चलता है दौर
शराब और मुर्गे का

Their voice is
drowned
In the auction bid-calls
Or in the burr of the saws.
Sonai, Sudni or Manchi
Lifting their grand-kids
Cry out
Even as they gather
Mahua[18], *tora*
Sal-seed or *chaar*,
What will become of our hungry bellies
Our thatched roofs
Why are you stripping us?

Her cry
Drowns
In the raucous buzz
Of trucks winding past
The Khursel ghat
Bound for Dhamtari
Raipur, Visakhapatnam.

Then a large chair
Visits their village
With its paraphernalia.
All get engaged in the *ghotul,*
Even the old and the elderly,

---

18 *Mahua* (Madhulika Indica), *tora* (kernel of Mahua), sal-seed and
chaar (an embellisher) are the major non-timber forest produces
in Bastar.

वापस जाने से पहले कुर्सी
धन्यवाद देना चाहती है
गाँव के पटेल को
कोटवार को, और सरपंच को भी
तब पता नहीं किधर से
दौड़ती-हाँपती आती है
सोनाय, सुदनी या कि मनची
अपने साथ घसीटते हुए
अपने नातियों को
और पूछ बैठती है:
''हम कहाँ से बीनें महुआ,
टोरा, सालबीज या चार,
लाएँ कहाँ से 'झाटी' और 'मेड़ा'
रूँधने को बाड़ी अपने
या आइजात की लकड़ी
राँधने को पेज
'सरगी' या 'करा' की पाटियाँ
और काँडा
कि बना सकें झोपड़ी
बचने के लिए धूप और बरसात से
जला सकें 'आँतरा'
बचने को शीत से

कि तंग करता है नाकेदार
छीन लेता है टँगिया
जारी करता है पीओआर
और लात-घूँसों से मारता है रेंजर...''

Busy to humour the chair
Mandri dance is organized
Followed by rounds of wine
And roasted chicken

Before returning back
The chair desires to thank
The *patel*[19] of the village
And the *kotwar*[20] and the sarpanch,
When from nowhere
Rushes in Sonai, breathless,
Sonai, Sudni or Manchi
Come dragging behind them
Their grand-kids
To ask:
From where should we gather
Mahua, tora, sal-seed or *chaar?*
From where should we gather
Jhaati or *meda*
To plaster our farmstead?
Or brushwood
To brew our *pej*[21]?
Sargi and *karra* planks
To build our hut
To shelter ourselves
From sun and rain
And raise a fire

---

19 Head-man.
20 A village-level quasi-formal constable.
21 Gruel.

बड़े इत्मीनान से सुनती है कुर्सी
और कहती है:
"जंगल काट डालोगे
तब जानते हो क्या होगा?
बरसात नहीं होगी
और तब पैदा नहीं कर सकोगे
'धान, कोदो या कुटकी'
मर जाओगे भूखे
बताओं,
क्या मरना है मंजूर?
क्या...?
इसीलिए मत काटो जंगल"

तभी हिड़मा या मँगलू
कहना चाहते हैं कुछ
कि कुर्सी
बैठ कर अपनी जीप में
अदृश्य हो जाती है
मुख्य सड़क की ओर
जाते हुए
कच्चे जंगली रास्ते में
और वह
अपनी निराश आँखों से देखती है
जब अपने नातियों की ओर
तब न जाने क्यों
वह सिहर उठती है
उसे उन आँखों में
कुतुहल की जगह दिखाई देती है आग
और दिखते हैं

To shield ourselves
from the cold?

The forest guard
Harasses us.
He confiscates our axe,
Issues a P.O.R,
And the ranger kicks us around.

The chair gives a patient hearing
And says:
If you fell the forest
Do you know what will happen?
Rain will fail
And you cannot raise paddy, *kodo* or *kutki*.
You will starve to death.
Tell me now
Would you like to die?
Speak…?
And so I say
Do not destroy the forest!

Hidma or Manglu
Would like to interject,
But the chair has
Boarded the jeep
And is gone
Out of view towards the main road
Along the kutcha pathway,
And when with
Disappointed eyes

फरसे की धार तेज करते लड़के
तब वह धीरे से दुहरी देती है गुरूमन्त्र:
"वन राष्ट्र की सम्पति है
इसकी हिफ़ाजत करना
हमारा नैतिक कर्तव्य है"

तभी उसकी निगाहें
बरबस ही फरसा के पेड़ की ओर
चली जाती हैं
जहाँ फूले हुए हैं
फरसा के लाल, गहरे लाल फूल।

She views her grand-kids,
For some reason
She shivers.
She sees not frolic
but fire in those eyes.
And she sees boys
Grinding the machete,
And then she slowly mutters
The Gurumantra:
Forests are the nation's assets
Protecting these
Is our moral duty!

Her eyes involuntarily
Turn towards the *farsa* tree[22]
That is in full bloom
With red, deep red flowers.

---

22 *Farasa* also means a battle-axe.

भ्रांति

गुजरती है
एक सड़क
एक लम्बी सड़क
बीचोंबीच बीहड़ों के

सड़क के किनारे
खड़े हैं वृक्ष
वृक्षों की हरीतिमा में
बेतरह लिपटी है लालिमा
हो गए धूसर

सड़क की धूल और ग़र्द से
सराबोर हैं
साल और सागौन के सारे दरख़्त
उनसे दूर
जंगल के अंदरूनी हिस्से में
खड़े ख़मोश
साल और सागौन
अब भी हरे हैं

खुसर-पुसर चल रही है
हरे वृक्ष पूछते हैं उनसे
तुम्हारा रंग
हमसे अलग क्यों है
हमारी ही बिरादरी के होने के बावजूद?

Misbelief

A road,
a long road
Passes through
the wilderness.

Trees stand
by the roadside.
The green foliage
Of the trees
Indifferently spotted
With red and grey.

The roadside dust
Has showered
The *sal* and teak crests.
Far away,
In the deep forest
Sal and teak
Are green still.

In whispers
Green trees query:
Why are you differently coloured
Despite being our kin?

निराश, बुझे स्वर में
छोटा सा उत्तर फेंकते हैं वे
मित्र! सड़क की धूल है वह
जिसने बदरंग किया है हमें
और अब
फैला रहे हैं भ्रांति
हमारे-तुम्हारे बीच।

Sad, in low voice
These toss up a brief reply:
Friend! The roadside dust
Has discoloured us!
And now
They are spreading
Misbelief
Between us!

पता नहीं कैसे

अभी
उस दिन हुए
ट्रक दुर्घटना में मरे
हम्मालों के ख़ून
सूख भी नहीं पाए हैं
सड़क पर से
सड़क पर पड़े गढ्ढों में
लबालब भर गया है लहू
जहाँ से उखड़ गयी है
गिट्टी और कोलतार

और फिर भी
भरी चली आ रही है ट्रकें लट्ठों से
ओवरलोड हैं
ट्रक मालिक को
कम समय में
ज़्यादा माल ढोना है
डीज़ल बहुत महँगा हो गया है

ट्रक पर लदे लट्ठों पर
बैठे हैं काले-कलूटे
अधनंगे बदन मज़दूर
'धुँगिया' मलते, बीड़ी का धुआँ उगलते
कभी 'लेजा' कभी 'चइतपरब' गाते
मज़दूर

Wonder How

In the truck mishap
The other day,
The blood of workhands
Who died
Has not yet dried
On the road;
Potholes on the road
Where gravel and tarmac
Have been washed away,
Are filled with blood.

Nevertheless
Trucks continue to ply
With their overload of logs!
The trucker must transport
As much in as short a time.
Diesel is so dear!

Perched on the logs
In the truck
Are darkly-besmeared workhands,
Grinding tobacco,
Puffing out the beedi-smoke,
Singing now *leja* now *chaitparab*[23]!

---

23 Merry songs.

सड़क के किनारे
होटलनुमा झोपड़ी में
बैठा मैं
उस रोज़ की घटना से
आतंकित, चुपचाप
भरी ट्रक में न बैठने का
मेरा निश्चय
प्रतीक्षा बस की

मज़दूर
जाने क्यों अब भी बैठे हैं
जहाँ के तहाँ
देख कर भी कि ख़ून के दाग़
जस के तस सड़क पर
बिछे हुए हैं
बेख़ौफ़ बैठे हैं मज़दूर
क्यों?
पता नहीं क्यों?
कैसे?
पता नहीं कैसे?

By the roadside
In a hut-like eatery
I, sitting,
Terrified by that mishap
Resolved silently
Never to ride a loaded truck.
I wait for a bus.

The workhands
Are nevertheless
Perched as before!
Even though the blood stains
On the road are loud,
Heedless they sit;
Why?
Wonder why!
How?
Wonder how!

वे नहरें

मेरे गाँवे के एक छोर पर
सिंचाई के लिये
खोदा गया है तालाब
तालाब से निकाली गयी हैं नहरें
नहरें, जो सीधे जाती हैं
एक नामी-गिरामी किसान के खेतों तक

उस तालाब से पानी
तभी भेजा जाता है बाहर
जब
उस किसान का होता है आदेश

या फिर तब
जब भर जाता है लबालब
वह तालाब
बरखा के पानी से
या फिर तब
जब मारना होता है मछलियाँ
ठेकेदार को
तब बेदर्दी से पानी
भेजा जाता है
बाहर तालाब के
तब किनारे खड़े लोग
सोचते रह जाते हैं
काश! यह पानी
बहा होता

Those Canals

In a corner of my village
A pond has been dug
For irrigation.
From the pond
Canals have been drawn,
That lead straight
To the lands of a Somebody.

The water from the ponds
Are let out
Only when
That Somebody ordains;

Or else then when
The pond is brim-full
With rainwater;
Or else then, when
The contractor
Choses to fish.

Water flows then mindlessly.
People standing on the bank
Sigh, if only this water
Had slaked our parched lands,
The harvest of hope would have

हमारे प्यासे खेतों पर
तो लहलहाती होतीं
फसलें उम्मीदों की
किन्तु
नहीं होता ऐसा
उम्मीदों के अंकुर भी
नहीं फूट पाते

वैसे तो
वे नहरें गुज़रती हैं
कई किसानों के खेतों के पास से
होती हुई
किन्तु वे नहरें
बीच में कहीं भी पानी देना
समझती हैं अपमान अपना

दूसरे किसानों से पूछता हूँ
जब उन नहरों की बात
मासूम-सा मिलता है उत्तर:
हमें पता नहीं
क्यों खोदी गयी हैं
ये नालियाँ (नहरें)
क्यों बनाया गया है
यह तालाब!

दरअसल भोले हैं बहुत
ये नादान!
ये नहरें और तालाब

Swayed in the breeze!
But
This does not happen;
Hope cannot so much as sprout.

The canals do pass by the lands
Of several farmers,
But the canals find it insulting
to water lands enroute.

When I ask these other farmers
Regarding the canals,
An innocent reply follows:
We have no idea why these
Canals were drawn
Or why the pond was dug!

These people
Are simpletons!
These canals and pond are
In the grip of the Somebody's fist.
They await signals
Of the masters.

It would be better
Perhaps
If the course of these canals
Is forced
Towards one's own and
everybody's land;

दोनों तो है
किसी की मुठ्ठी में बन्द
करती है ये प्रतीक्षा
अपने आक़ाओं के इशारों की

इसलिये
बेहतर होगा
यदि इन नहरों का मुँह
ज़बरन मोड़ लिया जाये
अपने-अपने
और हर किसी के
खेतों की ओर
या फिर
पाट दिया जाये यह गुलाम तालाब
मिट्टी से
सपाट बना दी जायें
वे तमाम नहरें
जो
हमारे खेतों के पास से
गुजर कर भी
हमारे खेतों को
पानी देना
समझती हैं
अपना अपमान।

Or else
The bonded-pond be filled up again
With earth,
And the canals
That pass by our fields
Yet deem it insulting
To water our lands
Be razed.

पलाश के बारे में

भई गुलमोहर!
तुम हो तो बड़े से पेड़
दो-चार फूल खिला कर
तुमने मोह लिया है
सब का मन
यानी हो गए हो स्थापित

तुम जैसे फूल तो
और पेड़ भी खिला सकते हैं
मसलन पलाश भी
और
छोटे-छोटे पौधे तो
तुम्हारी बनिस्बत
बहुत अच्छी फ़सलें देते हैं
बिना ज़्यादा जगह घेरे
और फिर
तुम्हारी इतनी बड़ी काया से
कभी कोई इमारती लकड़ी भी तो नहीं मिली
न मिलेगी
तुम खोखले जो हो
फिर भी लोग
बड़ी क़ीमतों में तुम्हें ख़रीद कर
रोपते हैं अपने घरों में
दरअसल तुम्हारे फूल
होते हैं बड़े रोमान्टिक
और फिर लोग फूल नहीं चाहते

About Palash[24]

Brother Gulmohar!
You sure are a huge tree
Putting forth a few flowers.
You have charmed
All hearts
And are firmly established.

Your kind of flowers
Are possible for others as well;
Palash, for instance;
And
Thanks to you
Small plants put forth great crop
Without requiring much space,
And then
For all your huge form
Never was any worthy timber got
Nor ever can be got from you,
Hollow as you are.
And yet, people pay high
To buy you and plant you at home.

Frankly your flowers
Are very romantic.
People perhaps do not need flowers.

---

24 L. *Butea Monosperma* a tree sacred to the tribes.

वरना पलाश क्या बुरा है?
कम से कम तुमसे अधिक तेज रंग का तो है
और बात यहीं साफ़ हो जाती है
और साफ हो जाती है
लोगों की नीयत भी

लोग घबराते हैं पलाश के तीखे रंग से
इसलिए लगाते हैं गुलमोहर
पुश्त-दर-पुश्त रोपा जा रहा है गुलमोहर
बग़ीचों में, घरों में
और पलाश
युगों से पड़ा है बीहड़ों में
किसी पड्यन्त्र का शिकार

Else what's wrong with *palash*, after all?
It has a hue much deeper than yours
And the point is clear here
And also clear in the people's mind –

They are terrified by the loud hue of palash,
And instead choose Gul Mohar
For parks and for homes.
Palash
Has been pushed to the wilderness for ages;
Victim of some conspiracy.

पलाश का समूचा पेड़

जंगल में खड़े
पलाश के पेड़ पर
खिले लाल-लाल फूलों को
देख कर उसने सोचा
उनमें से कुछ फूल तोड़ कर
भर लेगा अपनी 'ओली' में

दूसरे दिन वह पहुँचा
ऐन उसी जगह पर
वह आश्चर्य चकित था

कुछ वर्दियाँ
बन्दूकों की देख-रेख में
काट कर ले जा रही थीं
पलाश का समूचा पेड़

वह योच रहा था
किसने की है यह शिकायत
जबकि उसने
किसी से भी नहीं कही थी
अपने मन की बात।

Palash Tree

Viewing the deep red flowers
Of palash in the forest,
He thought
He could pluck some of them
And gather them in his drape.

The following day
He came bang to the
Same spot,
And was shocked!

Some uniforms
Under the watch of guns
Were felling
The entire tree of palash
to bear it away!

He wondered
Who must have reported,
For he had not shared
His desire
With anyone.

मत रो

मत रो बेटे।
भूख और प्यास पर
टूटती साँस पर
रोना ही है तो रो
गुम होते प्यार पर
ढहते विश्वास पर
दूर होती आस पर
इन्सानियत की लाश पर
रो... जी भर कर रो।

Weep Not

Weep not, son!
For hunger or thirst;
For fading breath;
If you must weep, weep
Over the fading of love,
The sinking of trust
The receding of hope
On the corpse of humanity
Weep, weep to your heart's fill!

जादू

सहसा
होने वाला है
एक जादू
इक्कीसवीं सदी में

आकाश
बजाएगा ताली
और
धरती हो जाएगी
हरी-भरी!

मिट जायेगी
भूख-प्यास
ढँक जायेगा तन
बन जायेंगे महल
हर ख़ास-ओ-आम के लिये

फिर मेरे बच्चे
क्यों होते हो हलकान
क्यों रोते हो
भूख-प्यास-बीमारी से

चुप बैठों दम साध कर
और जादू की करो प्रतीक्षा।

Magic

Suddenly
A magic
Is due to happen
In the twenty-first century!

The sky shall clap
And
The earth shall turn green!

Hunger and thirst shall
Vanish!
Bodies shall be
Clad!
Castles shall rise
For the high and the low!

Then why, dear children,
Do you fear?
Why do you cry
In hunger, thirst and sickness?

Sit quietly
And wait for the magic
To happen.

बाढ़

तुक नहीं
उफनती नदियों की प्रतिक्षा का
महज दिवास्वप्न है यह
नदियों में बाढ़ एकाएक
नहीं आ सकती
ऐसे में
जबकि वहाँ
नहीं है नदी कोई
बाढ़ के लिये नदी का होना तो
ज़रूरी है न?

और तुम नदी नहीं हो
भाई मेरे
एक बड़ी नदी बनने के लिए
पहले एक छोटी-सी धारा
तो बनना ही पड़ेगा

लेकिन याद रखना
यह भी कि
बरसाती धार
कभी भी निरंतर नहीं बहा करते
धार को अपनी गति,
भले ही वह धीमी हो
निरन्तर बनाए रखना होगा

वैसे तुम जानते तो होगे
एक धारा
जो बहती है निरन्तर

Flood

Meaningless
To wait for rivers in spate;
Mere utopian dream, this.
Rivers do not flood of a sudden.
They cannot flood
In places where
There is no river.
For flood, you need a river,
Right?

And you, brother,
Are no river;
To be a large river
You first need to be a stream.

And remember this:
Seasonal streams
Are never perennial.
A stream must sustain its flow,
Never mind the flow is slow.

You may be aware of
A thin stream
That flows in a sustained way
Cutting the edges
It flows persistently.
Gradually

तटों का कटाव करती
चली जाती है वही
फिर धीरे-धीरे वह अपनी
इसी प्रक्रिया के चलते
बन जाती है
एक छोटा-सा नाला

दरअसल
उसमें धैर्य होता है बड़ा
कटाव की यह प्रक्रिया
कालान्तर में
बना देती है उसे
एक छोटी नदी
फिर वही छोटी नदी
बदल जाती है
एक बड़ी नदी में
तब कई नदियाँ
आ कर मिल जाती हैं उससे
राह में
वे नदियाँ
जो गुज़र रही होती हैं
उसी प्रक्रिया से
उनके अतीत में भी होती है
वही एक छोटी-सी धारा,
वही अनगढ़ नाला
और तभी सम्भव हो पाता है
बाढ़ का आना
तब टूट जाते हैं
तटबन्ध
डूब जाते हैं
आसपास के गाँव
मच जाता है हाहाकार।

It becomes a brook
It has great courage.
The erosion at the edges
Makes it in course of time
A small river,
And then this small river
Grows large,
Then several streams
Come and join it.
The rivers on the way
Share the same past.
A small stream
Stubborn stream
And only then
Can flood be;
And then, the banks fall
The villages around submerge
And then there is an outcry!

उत्तर दो

सुदनी क्यों रोती है बोड़ू,
बिलख-बिलख कर आँख सुजाती?
सोनू क्योंकर तड़प रहा है,
मनची है क्यों आँख चुराती?
हे दरबारी उत्तर दो
सही-सही तुम उत्तर दो।

शाल, खैर, सागौन कहाँ हैं,
कौन रहा भर अपना घर?
महुए की वह महक किधर है,
ट्रकें खड़ी किनकी छाती पर?
पहरेदारो उत्तर दो
सही-सही तुम उत्तर दो।

कौन है क़ातिल फगनी का,
यशोदा की इज़्जत किसने लूटी?
सब-कुछ बिल्कुल साफ़ है लेकिन
क्यों न यह ख़ामोशी टूटी?
निर्भीक तराजू उत्तर दो
सही-सही तुम उत्तर दो।
लोहे की वह खान बिकी तो
घर में बाक़ी नहीं है छुरी?

Answer, please

Why does Sudni cry, O Uncle,
Wailing, her eyes a-swollen?
Why is Sonu writhing,
And Manchi avoiding eye-contact?
Oh Officer, answer please
And pray, speak the truth.

Where are *Sal, Khair*[25], Teak?
Who is hoarding them?
Where is the fragrance of *mahua*?
On whose bodies
Are these trucks parked?
O guards, answer please
And pray, speak the truth.

Who killed Fagni,
Who raped Yashoda?
Everything seems very clear
Why then this silence?
Fearless scales[26], answer please
And pray, speak the truth.

---

25 L. *Senegalia catechu*, a species of tree.
26 Of judiciary.

तीर नहीं बन सकता क्या
फिर कैसी चुप्पी कैसी दूरी?
वन-उपवन गिरी उत्तर दो
सही-सही तुम उत्तर दो।

The iron-ore mines were sold;
But is there no dagger left at home?
Can an arrow not be crafted?
Why this silence, why this distance?
Forests and hills, answer please
And pray, speak the truth.

मँड़िया का पेज

अटपट है गरमी, लो धूप हुई तेज
ऐसे में भाता है, मँड़िया का पेज।

बड़ा बुरा हाल है, गरमी के मारे
पहुँचाये ठण्डक तब, हियरा के द्वारे
आमा की चटनी हो, अमटाया पेज ।।

डोकरा हो डोकरी कि, नोनी या नोना
सभी ढाल लेते हैं, दोने पर दोना
नहीं कोई दूजा ज्यों, मँड़िया का पेज।।

घर आये पहुना को, चाय नहीं भाती
पेज भरे दोना को, अँखियाँ ललचातीं
जुड़ाता है जियरा को, मँड़िया का पेज।।

Millet Gruel

Summer is hot, the sun is scorching
At such a time, millet-gruel is soothing.

The scorching summer is awful.
Cool enters the heart with
Mango-chutney and sour gruel.

Old man or old woman, boy or girl,
All down it, leaf-cup over cup,
Nothing can rival the millet-gruel.

The guest come home is averse to tea;
His eyes long for a bowl of gruel;
Fellowship flourishes on millet-gruel!

इन्सान आज का

इनसानियत की ओढ़ चादर
इन्सान को ही छल रहे
भगवान का ही नाम ले कर
भगवान को ही छल रहे।

आया ये कैसा दौर देखो
खूं के प्यासे हो गये
हैवानियत की शक्ल में
इन्सान कैसे ढल रहे।

क्या थे, क्या हम हो गये
फ़िरक़ा परस्ती के सबब
दिल का सुकूं जाता रहा
विश्वास कैसे जल रहे।

Man Today

Donning a stole of humanity
To dupe fellow beings
In the holy name of God
Trying to dupe very God!

O what an age this is!
Thirst relates blood!
In the devil's mould, behold,
How we are re-shaping.

What we were, what we've made of ourselves
Pursuing exclusiveness
Calm is leaking out of the heart,
Trust is burning out!

www.ingramcontent.com/pod-product-compliance
Lightning Source LLC
Chambersburg PA
CBHW051237130726
47988CB00001B/383